I0414339

Inspirational Sentiments
to Become a Better Person

A Starter Manual by
Joseph N. DeLuca, MD, PhD

Strategic Book Publishing and Rights Co.

Strategic Book Publishing and Rights Co.
12620 FM 1960, Suite A4-507
Houston, TX 77065
www.sbpra.com

ISBN: 978-1-61897-386-3

Book Design: Suzanne Kelly

Dedication

I dedicate this book to my grandmother, Anna Gioffre. She did private duty nursing in several New York City hospitals, taking care of extremely ill children. When I was in elementary school she would ask me to write a note to the particular child she was caring for, telling him or her that I knew they would be feeling better soon and getting well. When she would give the note to the child she was caring for she would enclose a Baby Ruth candy bar, and tell the child it came from me. After doing this for several years I began to realize that my grandmother was an extremely caring, compassionate person, and I thought that when I grew up, it would be nice if I could be just like her.

My fantasy is that some day soon, as a volunteer, I will be able to play with children who are terminally ill, and when I am through playing with them, I will give them a Baby Ruth candy bar, and I will tell them it came from my grandmother.

THANK YOU, GRANDMA.

About the Author

Dr. Joseph N. DeLuca is a board certified clinical psychologist who is also a primary care physician. He advocates the mind/body concept and focuses on health enhancement and preventative medicine. He uses a multi-dimensional approach that utilizes spirituality, exercise, nutrition, and non-traditional approaches to enhance health and well being, as well as traditional Western medicine.

Becoming a Better Person: A Starter Manual

All of the following are things that the author has read, heard in lectures, or personally experienced. There are undoubtedly hundreds of things an individual can do in his or her quest to become a better person. The references listed at the end of this book are the main sources for the recommendations included here. There are no doubt hundreds of books written by philosophers, theologians, psychologists, and others, which greatly expand on one's quest to become a better person. However, the thought was to list a few basics (a starter manual) so that one can use the recommendations that follow to practice a few of these ideas each day in his or her quest to become a better person.

Perhaps the Best Way to Use This Manual Is as Follows

If, for example, the sentiment of the day you choose is "Enable the Dreams of Others," the most meaningful way to implement this would be to, on the blank page that follows, write down whose dream you want to enable, what that person's dream is, and what the different things are that you can do to enable that person's dream. It can be something very simple, such as offering a word of encouragement or praise for that person's journey toward their goal. Things only become meaningful if one attempts to implement the idea that they believe is a good one.

Joseph N. DeLuca, MD, PhD

IT IS BETTER TO BE NICE THAN TO BE RIGHT

Several years ago, I was working with two girls in the elite tennis program for individuals who were highly ranked in their age group. I was working with them as a sport psychologist and, while observing them practicing with each other, one of the girls felt that the other was frequently calling her ball out, while she thought it was in. These girls, who had been very good friends up until that point, ended up no longer being friends because the one accused the other of being a cheater. They did not speak with each other for several weeks. During one of our sport psychology sessions we came upon the theme of better to be nice than to be right. What this means, in the case of these girls, is that the girl who felt the other girl was cheating could have best handled the situation by simply saying, "Well it looked in to me, but you certainly were closer to the ball and I guess if it looked out it was probably was out," and to no longer get suckered into a confrontational mode. In an important tournament a referee would be calling the ball in and out and it would be out of their hands. Of course it is good to be right, but it is better to be nice about it. If someone says something that you feel is incorrect, offer what you feel is the correct information in a way that is not filled with hostility or vindictiveness.

Whenever anyone is critical or confrontational, one method that is helpful is called "Reflective Listening." This simply means that you listen carefully to what a person is saying and reflect back to them what you understand they are saying and how they feel, and you do not offer any evaluation, criticism, or defense of your own position. This is usually a good approach because most people really just want to be understood, as opposed to being given well-meaning advice.

Read: *Getting the Love You Want* by H. Hendrix

THINGS I CAN DO TO IMPLEMENT THE PREVIOUS SENTIMENT

JUST SHUT UP—LEARNING TO LISTEN

People want to be understood and not to be given constructive criticism, unless they specifically ask for it. Everyone really just wants to have their feelings and thoughts understood without any evaluation from the listener as to whether the listener thinks these thoughts and feelings are okay, good, or not okay. People really do feel better when others are trying to listen and understand their true feelings. There is a tendency for men to want to offer constructive criticism to women as a solution when a woman is upset. However, women really just want to be understood and not told what to do to fix the problem. To be a good listener requires patience, perseverance, and the ability to not interject one's own opinions about what the speaker is saying. The skill of reflective listening is essential. An individual listens carefully to what the other person is saying, even if it is a criticism, and does not get suckered into defending oneself or criticizing back. The goal is to reflect back to the speaker what you understand they are saying and feeling.

Read: *Getting the Love You Want* by H. Hendrix

THINGS I CAN DO TO IMPLEMENT THE PREVIOUS SENTIMENT

THE JOY OF BUSTING YOUR BUTT

As a person who was born without any natural ability in anything, whenever I achieved something, the joy that went along with it was overwhelmingly tremendous. Many people are fortunate to be either intellectually gifted or in other ways extremely talented, and they are often complimented by others for their achievements. Many of them, however, must feel that what they have achieved was not very difficult. Which reminds me of a line from the movie *Legally Blonde*, when someone says to the main character, "You got into Harvard Law School?" and she replies, "Oh, is that supposed to be hard?"

THINGS I CAN DO TO IMPLEMENT THE PREVIOUS SENTIMENT

BE EXTRA KIND

Whenever an obese unattractive woman or man walks by me I make sure to give her or him the biggest smile and biggest good morning or hello that I can muster. I feel we should do this sort of thing to the people who need it the most. Remember, a single smile or hello can make a person's day and be so mood enhancing. Research has shown that significantly overweight people get less help with things than people who are more physically attractive. Also, research shows that with equivalent credentials people that are overweight or unattractive are less likely to get the job than a person who is more attractive. Therefore, the bottom line is to reach out to those people who may be shunned or responded to in a less than a positive manner.

THINGS I CAN DO TO IMPLEMENT THE PREVIOUS SENTIMENT

LOLLIPOPS AND "MORE"

Recently my granddaughter, Molly, age two and a half, bruised her knee. She looked up at me and said, "A lollipop would make it better." About a week prior, my granddaughter, Micaela, age one and a half, was playing a game with me in which I would chase her and then she would hide. Upon my finding where she was hiding, she would say "More, more."

Well, the point of the above is that we need to collect our lollipops and our "more" because these are the little things that give us pleasure and help us better navigate through the bumps in the road that we experience each day. So, make a list of what would make you feel good if you had more of it, and what, for you, are your lollipops and mores.

THINGS I CAN DO TO IMPLEMENT THE PREVIOUS SENTIMENT

REDREAM

Everyone had childhood dreams. My dream as a child, growing up in the Bronx, was to become a baseball player for the New York Yankees. However, when I was cut from my high school baseball team three years in a row, the dream was shattered, and I was unbearably heartbroken. Another dream that I had while growing up, since I was enamored of science, was to become a physicist. However, after taking, during my first year of college, calculus, physics, and chemistry, I discovered that I had absolutely no aptitude for science, and again experienced great disappointment and felt completely heartbroken. Approximately two years later, upon walking into the university library one night, I discovered a sculpture in the hallway, which was of a person's hand holding a brain. I then thought, "Wow, the human brain is the most complex thing in the universe." To pursue a career that would involve dealing with the human brain would be a truly exciting adventure that I felt great passion about. I therefore pursued a career in psychology, which has worked out very well. A few weeks later, while walking by that same piece of sculpture, I discovered that I had misinterpreted the sculpture and it was really meant to portray God's hand holding the creation of the earth. However, it was good that I saw it as I did, as it started a new dream for me.

The point of the above is that no matter what dreams you may have had that have been shattered or unobtainable, you can always redream. You can always find another dream to connect with in a passionate way. So, the word on the street is "keep redreaming."

THINGS I CAN DO TO IMPLEMENT THE PREVIOUS SENTIMENT

YOU CAN'T SUCCEED IN ACCOMPLISHING A GOAL IF YOU DON'T GET RID OF THE EMOTIONAL REASONS WHY YOU ARE NOT SUCCEEDING

Many years ago, I worked with two world-class athletes as a clinical sports psychologist. Both had established a world record, one in swimming and one in track and field, and each of their coaches said to them, at some point, "What has gotten into you that has enabled you to train with such intensity?" Each of them said to their coach, "It is not what got into me, it is what got out of me".

Everyone realizes the advantages of obtaining ideal body weight, and they know what they should do, but most people have trouble actually doing it. It may well be that there is a psychological reason within most people that makes them resistant to doing the things that will bring their weight down to an ideal level. We know there is an epidemic of overweight individuals in the United States, where approximately two out of three people are overweight, and about one out of three children are obese. Obtaining your ideal body weight enhances physical and emotional well-being. If you are finding it difficult to do the things that will bring your weight into the ideal range, talk to a counselor or psychologist about underlying factors that you may not be aware of that are interfering with this.

Read: *It's Not What You're Eating, It's What Eating You* (audio book) by Janet Greeson, PhD

THINGS I CAN DO TO IMPLEMENT THE PREVIOUS SENTIMENT

BE GRATEFUL FOR ALL OF THE THINGS YOU HAVE EXPERIENCED IN THE PAST, CURRENTLY, AND ANTICIPATE FOR THE FUTURE

This basically means that each day one should quietly say to oneself, or to another, what they are grateful for. It might be having loving and caring parents, having the opportunities for a good education, or having been born with special abilities, aptitudes, or talents, or having been born in an environment of safety and security. Expressing one's gratitude to another for things that they have done to enhance your well-being is extremely desirable. Gratitude is simply an acknowledgement of those individuals' efforts to contribute to your well-being. Thanking someone for what they do that is helpful or pleasing to you is one of the five languages of love.

Read: *The Five Love Languages* by Gary Chapman

THINGS I CAN DO TO IMPLEMENT THE PREVIOUS SENTIMENT

DEVELOP THE ABILITY TO FORGIVE OTHERS FOR WHAT THEY HAVE DONE THAT WAS HURTFUL TO YOU AND THE ABILITY TO FORGIVE YOURSELF FOR THINGS THAT YOU HAVE DONE THAT WERE HURTFUL TO OTHERS

The ability to let go of hurts that you have experienced or perpetrated upon others is one of the keys to happiness and well-being. To harbor hostility toward others for things that you feel were harmful or hurtful to you increases the probability that you will experience depression and medical illnesses. It is also necessary that you be contrite and feel appropriate guilt for things you have done that were hurtful to others. The important thing is that you recognize your behaviors and attempt to take corrective action to rectify. If a higher source can forgive us for inappropriate behavior, who are we to say that we cannot be forgiving of others? The ability to look at what caused a person's past hurtful behaviors is important. People often behave badly because of insecurity, dependency, anxiety, depression, feelings of inadequacy, intimidation, etc. We need to respond to the underlying feelings that are causing the surface behavior so that we can truly understand others' difficult behaviors.

THINGS I CAN DO TO IMPLEMENT THE PREVIOUS SENTIMENT

ENABLING THE DREAMS OF OTHERS

One of our main goals should be to figure out each day what we can do to make someone else's life better and especially to help make someone else's dream become a reality. We all know the dreams, hopes, and aspirations of our family and loved ones, but how often do we make a significant contribution to making those dreams a reality? A good thing to do each day is to come up with a specific act or behavior that will help enable the dreams of a person you care about.

Read: *The Last Lecture* by Randy Pausch

THINGS I CAN DO TO IMPLEMENT THE PREVIOUS SENTIMENT

LOOK FOR THE POSITIVE IN EVERYONE

Everyone is a collection of positive and negative traits and behaviors. It is more helpful to others when you point out what is good or positive about them. This works a lot better than harping on the negative because when you focus on the negative people become defensive and often hostile and rebellious. Helping a person build on their strengths by praising the positive yields a better result than focusing on their weak points. Positive reinforcement always works better than negative reinforcement. Trying to teach by humiliation never quite produces the desired result. You want to enhance the ego of others rather than damage or take away from their strengths.

Read: All of Wayne Dyer's books

THINGS I CAN DO TO IMPLEMENT THE PREVIOUS SENTIMENT

REPUTATION IS WHAT OTHERS THINK OF YOU; CHARACTER IS WHAT GOD KNOWS ABOUT YOU

It is important that you work on your character and not on trying to make others have a positive image of you. It is what is inside of you that counts, not your external behavior. People often have a facade of nice behavior that covers up their hostilities, prejudices, and bias. One needs to become aware of his or her inner frailties and work on those more than on the cover-up or façade.

THINGS I CAN DO TO IMPLEMENT THE PREVIOUS SENTIMENT

GET IN TOUCH WITH YOUR BODY

This means realizing that the mind and body are one unit and every part of you is connected and influences every other part of you. Your physical well-being influences your mental and emotional states as well as vice versa. Therefore, working on regular exercise, at least twenty minutes a day, five days a week, will not only build new brain cells, but will also alleviate tension and stress, as well as enhancing the well-being of every organ system in your body. Exercise helps prevent every major medical problem. It also slows down the progression of medical problems that a person may already have.

Read: Books on sport psychology

THINGS I CAN DO TO IMPLEMENT THE PREVIOUS SENTIMENT

THE POWER OF TOUCH

Touch is the most basic way of communicating with another person. It can communicate love, concern, and any positive emotion. It is the most reassuring of all the ways of communication. Practicing the art of touch with those you care about will enhance their well-being as well as yours.

THINGS I CAN DO TO IMPLEMENT THE PREVIOUS SENTIMENT

Joseph N. DeLuca, MD, PhD

TRUST YOUR GUT FEELINGS—FIRST IMPRESSIONS

We need to rely on our emotional reaction to people and situations because our brain is picking up information that we may not be conscious of that is indicating whether we are having a positive or negative reaction to a particular place, person, or situation. A person emits many cues that are picked up by others on a subconscious level, which then leads to an emotional response to that individual. This is not to say that rational thinking should not be blended into our first impressions before acting upon them. However, it does mean that we should rely on gut impressions as being the prime source of information about a particular place, person, or situation.

Read: Blink by Malcolm Gladwell

THINGS I CAN DO TO IMPLEMENT THE PREVIOUS SENTIMENT

HAVE THE COURAGE TO BE A NOBODY

You should never do anything for the sake of applause, approval, notoriety, fame, or fortune. You should do it because it is basically a good thing to do. Do good work and if others give you positive feedback for your efforts, that is a good thing. The goal is to never do something for the purpose of approval or reward.

Read: *Franny and Zooey* by J.D. Salinger

THINGS I CAN DO TO IMPLEMENT THE PREVIOUS SENTIMENT

IF YOU THINK YOU CAN OR IF YOU THINK YOU CAN'T—
YOU ARE RIGHT!

This means that your body can only do what your brain believes it can do or gives it permission to do. Your body is not likely to respond in a positive manner, no matter what your goal is, if you believe that it is going to be too difficult. Place a limit on how far you can go or what you can accomplish, and your brain will not let your body go beyond that level. For example: if an eighth-grade baseball player thinks the highest skill level he can obtain is to make his high school baseball team then his brain is not going to let his body achieve any higher level of skill because it does not believe it can go beyond that level. Placing limitations on yourself locks you in to not being able to achieve any further progress.

Read: Any book on sport psychology

THINGS I CAN DO TO IMPLEMENT THE PREVIOUS SENTIMENT

DO A STRETCH

Each day you should attempt to extend yourself in some way that is good but uncomfortable. So if it is a good thing to say hello to your newly moved-in next-door neighbor, but you feel uncomfortable about it, do it anyway. Do a stretch.

THINGS I CAN DO TO IMPLEMENT THE PREVIOUS SENTIMENT

ASK FOR HELP

Many people are reluctant to ask for help for fear that they will be looked upon as ignorant, inadequate, helpless, or be the subject of ridicule or rejection. It takes more ego strength to recognize when you are having a problem and to reach out and ask for help than it does to deny to oneself or others that there is any kind of difficulty.

THINGS I CAN DO TO IMPLEMENT THE PREVIOUS SENTIMENT

FOCUS ON THE SEARCH FOR MEANING

Meaning basically involves what is important to you. What is meaningful will certainly vary according to one's stage in life. Finding meaning in your relationships, in your work, in your causes is very important and it is paramount that you be very much in touch with what is meaningful to you. There is evidence that loss of meaning in one's life is correlated with loss of spiritual well-being. It is possible to find meaning even in tragic circumstances. Meaning can take the form of knowing what you are responsible for. Spirituality and meaning tend to go hand in hand. Try to understand what one's place in the universe is, where you are from, and where you are going, in an attempt to tie together the big question. Faith in a higher power may also be what is meaningful to a person. Again, what you care about, what you love, or a cause you believe in is meaningful. Viewing life as having meaning changes what you believe in and what you attempt to create.

Read: *Man's Search for Meaning* by Viktor Frankl

THINGS I CAN DO TO IMPLEMENT THE PREVIOUS SENTIMENT

IF ONLY I WOULD HAVE/IF ONLY I SHOULD HAVE

Everyone, no doubt, has had experiences that they look back upon and feel that if only they could change the way they handled it, the outcome might have been different, or at the very least, they would not be plagued with guilt that they carry around because of it.

THINGS I CAN DO TO IMPLEMENT THE PREVIOUS SENTIMENT

PLAY WITH BABIES, PLAY WITH PETS

It enhances our well-being to be in touch with pure innocence. Babies, puppies, kittens, and other young creatures are pretty much the essence of innocence. Interacting with this enhances our sense of wellness.

THINGS I CAN DO TO IMPLEMENT THE PREVIOUS SENTIMENT

OBSERVE AND BE TOUCHED BY
THE CARING BEHAVIOR OF OTHERS

In his books and lectures, Wayne Dyer has indicated that simply by observing the caring behavior of others, as well as being the recipient or doer of caring behavior, increases our serotonin. Serotonin is a neurotransmitter that helps modulate anxiety and depression.

THINGS I CAN DO TO IMPLEMENT THE PREVIOUS SENTIMENT

EVEN THE SMALLEST ACT OF KINDNESS
CAN TURN A PERSON'S LIFE AROUND

It doesn't take more than a simple caring word, gesture, look, or act to profoundly touch a person's heart and make things go better for them for the rest of their life.

THINGS I CAN DO TO IMPLEMENT THE PREVIOUS SENTIMENT

FIND THE BEAUTY IN EVERYONE

Everyone has positive aspects. If you look deeply enough, everyone is quite beautiful.

THINGS I CAN DO TO IMPLEMENT THE PREVIOUS SENTIMENT

COURAGE

Everyone has had moments in their life when they were afraid of doing or saying the right thing for fear of criticism, retaliation, embarrassment, humiliation, and/or rejection. However, the ability to have courage is a skill. Like any skill, it takes practice, practice, practice. There is a concept called behavioral rehearsal, in which an individual practices what he or she would like to say in the manner that he or she would like to say it to the person involved. Behavioral rehearsal reduces the anxiety that goes with expressing one's true feelings.

THINGS I CAN DO TO IMPLEMENT THE PREVIOUS SENTIMENT

GRIEVING

Everyone has experienced losses, whether it be the loss of a parent, the loss of a loved one, the loss of a valued relationship, the loss of a childhood or adolescent dream, or a loss involving career, financial, or medical issues. One of the keys to dealing with loss or grief is to express the feelings you would have liked to have said to the person that you are grieving. Get out those feelings by expressing them verbally or in writing, even though the person may not be around to receive them.

THINGS I CAN DO TO IMPLEMENT THE PREVIOUS SENTIMENT

QUIT WHINING

Everyone has situations that are disappointing or upsetting, and there is a lot of moaning and groaning going on. The problem is that whining doesn't make anything better. It doesn't change history or circumstances. It does makes all three neurotransmitters primarily involved in mood—dopamine, norepinephrine, and serotonin—go down hill, and it increases depression and anxiety. Whining is never the solution to handling a situation that is worrisome or disappointing. The key is to focus on what is good in one's life and build on that. Also, coming up with a plan to deal with whatever one is bothered by is crucial. There is evidence that coming up with a plan to deal with something that is a concern greatly reduces the anxiety connected with it, and of course the most important thing is to implement the plan.

THINGS I CAN DO TO IMPLEMENT THE PREVIOUS SENTIMENT

A REPLAY—A DO-OVER

Difficult circumstances from your past can be adjusted to more adequately by replaying, either in one's mind or by acting it out, how you would have liked the situation to turn out.

THINGS I CAN DO TO IMPLEMENT THE PREVIOUS SENTIMENT

LISTEN TO THE QUIET—HEAR THE SILENCE

This really just comes down to learning to be sensual. Meditation, where you focus on a particular part of your body, your breathing, or a particular sound or image, is extremely helpful in achieving the sensation of peaceful sensuality.

THINGS I CAN DO TO IMPLEMENT THE PREVIOUS SENTIMENT

MAKE SOMEONE SMILE—HAVE A SENSE OF HUMOR

Being able to look at oneself and others with a sense of humor is probably paramount to having a good day. Try not to take oneself so seriously. Having humorous jokes to share with others each day is really a good thing to do. Making someone else smile is really a good deed. Practicing seeing what is humorous about oneself or actions is really goal number one.

THINGS I CAN DO TO IMPLEMENT THE PREVIOUS SENTIMENT

CONTINUING EDUCATION

In order to prevent our brains from aging and eventually coming down with dementia, we need to be involved in continuing education. This ideally involves new learning, such as studying a new language, a musical instrument, or any other form of continuing education, like taking classes, reading, etc. Research has clearly shown that new learning, which can and should be joyful, significantly contributes to the health of the brain.

THINGS I CAN DO TO IMPLEMENT THE PREVIOUS SENTIMENT

A STRANGER IS JUST A MEMBER OF YOUR FAMILY
THAT YOU HAVE NOT MET YET

In one of Mitch Albom's books, the above is a direct quote from one of the characters. It is true that we are all members of one family even though on the surface we may appear, and sometimes act, quite different. We all have the same inner concerns, dreams, aspirations, conflicts, etc. Taking an understanding approach to strangers is really just like dealing with a family member.

THINGS I CAN DO TO IMPLEMENT THE PREVIOUS SENTIMENT

COMMUNICATE WITH EACH OTHER

Many years ago I was sitting at my desk in my office and I had this image of a friend of mine that I had not seen in several years, and who lived a thousand miles away, dialing my telephone number. Several seconds later my telephone rang and it was him. I had to believe that I felt his intent to communicate with me, even though I was not aware of any reason why I should have been thinking of him or why I thought he would want to contact me. We have all probably had similar experiences in our lifetime. Many times I have thought of a former patient I had not seen in years, and then the next day I would see on the schedule that patient's name. Again, I think the take away is that we can feel when someone is thinking of us, even though they may be thousands of miles away. When we think of someone that we have known at any stage of our life in a positive caring way, that person will feel it on some level. It is a good thing to think about people that we wish well or care about, knowing that in some way they may feel us thinking about them.

THINGS I CAN DO TO IMPLEMENT THE PREVIOUS SENTIMENT

LET OTHERS HELP YOU ENABLE YOUR DREAMS

While the ultimate goal is to contribute to the goals and dreams of others, it really is a sign of strength to let others know what your particular dreams and goals are so that they can be supportive or helpful in one or more ways. You may want to write down whom you want to be made aware of your goals and dreams on the next page, and perhaps what they could contribute to your progress. It really is a sign of strength and not of weakness to solicit the help of others in the pursuit of positive goals.

THINGS I CAN DO TO IMPLEMENT THE PREVIOUS SENTIMENT

GOOD NEWS

Make a list of all of the things that have happened in your life that you would consider "good news," whether they came in the form of a letter, an email, or a verbal communication. Each day, take at least one experience of "good news," sit down and close your eyes, and re-experience the emotion that went with the learning of the "good news."

THINGS I CAN DO TO IMPLEMENT THE PREVIOUS SENTIMENT

Readings

Healthy Aging by Dr. Andrew Weil

The Power of Intention by Wayne Dyer

Inspiration, Your Ultimate Calling by Wayne Dyer

There is a Spiritual Solution to Every Problem by Wayne Dyer

The Biology of Transcendence by Joseph Chilton Pearce

Soul, Mind, Body Medicine by Dr. Zhi Gang Sha

The Heart Speaks by Mimi Guanieri

Many Lives, Many Masters by Dr. Brian Weiss

Just One More Day by Mitch Albom

The Five People You Meet in Heaven by Mitch Albom

Tuesdays with Morrie by Mitch Albom

Have a Little Faith by Mitch Albom

The Heart's Code by Dr. Paul Pearsall

The Secret by Rhonda Byrne

The Seven Spiritual Laws of Success by Deepak Chopra

Reinventing the Body, Resurrecting the Soul by Deepak Chopra

A New Earth: Awakening to Your Life's Purpose by Eckhart Tolle

The Last Lecture by Randy Pausch

The Biology of Belief by Bruce Lipton

Outliers: The Story of Success by Malcolm Gladwell

Blink by Malcolm Gladwell

Man's Search for Meaning by Viktor Frankl

"Hard Work Beats Talent" by Kevin Durant

"Psychosocial and Spiritual Domains of Palliative Care," lecture by William Brettbans, MD

The New Toughness Training for Sports by James E. Loehr

Exploring Sport & Exercise Psychology by Judy L. Van Raalte, Britton W. Brewer

The Mental Athlete by Kay Porter

Talent is Overrated by Geoff Colvin

The Sport Psychologist Handbook by Shane Murphy

The Five Love Languages by Gary Chapman

Getting the Love You Want by H. Hendrix

Franny & Zooey by J.D. Salinger

It's Not What You're Eating, It's What Eating You by Janet Greeson, PhD

Acknowledgements

I am very grateful to my friend, Nucci Cento, for her inspiration, guidance, and support. Without her help this book would not have come to pass.

I wish to thank my wife, Dr. Penny DeLuca for her advice regarding editing, Susan Squarey for her enthusiastic support and suggestions regarding design of a front cover and Mark Gardberg for advice regarding publishing alternatives. In addition, I wish to thank all of you who felt the idea of this book was a good one that could be helpful to people of all ages.

I also wish to thank Karen Boble for her typing and re-typing of the manuscript until I got it right.

www.ingramcontent.com/pod-product-compliance
Lightning Source LLC
Chambersburg PA
CBHW081236280526
45787CB00006B/2682